1 MONTH OF
FREE
READING

at
www.ForgottenBooks.com

By purchasing this book you are eligible for one month membership to ForgottenBooks.com, giving you unlimited access to our entire collection of over 1,000,000 titles via our web site and mobile apps.

To claim your free month visit:
www.forgottenbooks.com/free792357

ISBN 978-0-484-18686-5
PIBN 10792357

THE LATTER-DAY SAINTS'
MILLENNIAL STAR.
[Established 1840.]

*"Good nature, like a bee, collects its honey from every herb;
ill-nature, like a spider, sucks poison from the sweetest flower.*

No. 5 Vol. LXIX.   Thursday, January 31, 1907.   Price One Penny.

THE LATTER-DAY SAINTS AND THE WORLD.

By Elder William A. Morton.

(Concluded from page 38.)

THE WORLD:—Do you claim to have received authority from
the Lord to preach the Gospel and administer in the ordinances
thereof?

Latter-day Saints:—We do. The Lord has in these last days restored, through the ministering of angels, both the Aaronic and
the Melchisedek Priesthood, empowering His servants to preach
the Gospel, baptize repentant believers for the remission of their
sins, confirm them members in His Church, and by prayer and the
imposition of hands call down upon them the Holy Ghost.

The World:—Must a man be called of God and divinely appointed
before he can preach acceptably the Gospel of Jesus Christ?

Latter-day Saints:—He must, as the Apostle Paul and others
will testify.

TESTIMONY OF PAUL.

The World:—Paul, do you consider it absolutely necessary in
order for a man to preach the Gospel and administer in its ordinances, that he be called of God and ordained by those holding
divine authority?

Paul:—I do. In every dispensation of the world the Lord

has chosen certain men to represent Him among the people. These He called, either by His own voice or by the voice of His servants whom He had previously chosen.

The World:—Can you cite us a few examples of the calling of men to the ministry?

Paul:—I can. The Lord called Noah to be a preacher of righteousness to the people of his generation; and when they would not hearken to the testimony of his authorized servant, the Lord destroyed them from the earth. Abraham, Isaac and Jacob were called in like manner for the work which the Lord had appointed them?

The World:—How were they called?

Paul:—They were called by direct revelation from heaven, the Lord speaking to them by His own voice. To Abraham He said: "Get thee out of thy country, and from thy kindred, and from thy father's house, unto a land that I will show thee: and I will make of thee a great nation, and I will bless thee, and make thy name great and thou shalt be a blessing; * * * and in thee shall all families of the earth be blessed." (Gen. 12: 1-3.) Isaac and Jacob were called in a similar manner. (Gen. 26: 2-5; 28: 10-15.)

The World:—Would it be improper for a man to preach the Gospel and administer its ordinances without his having been divinely commissioned to do so?

Paul:—It would, indeed. No man has a right to take such honor unto himself except he be called of God, as was Aaron. Permit me to read a couple of extracts from my epistle to the Romans and that to the Hebrews. This is what I said: "How then shall they call on him in whom they have not believed? and how shall they believe in him of whom they have not heard? and how shall they hear without a preacher? and how shall they preach except they be sent?" (Rom. 10: 14, 15.) "And no man taketh this honor unto himself, but he that is called of God, as was Aaron." (Heb. 5: 4.)

The World:—How was Aaron called to the ministry?

Paul:—He was called of the Lord through the Prophet Moses. As you well know, the Lord spoke to Moses out of the burning bush, commissioning him to go on a mission to Egypt and deliver therefrom the children of Israel. Moses reminded the Lord that he had an impediment in his speech, when the Lord said to him: "Is not Aaron the Levite thy brother? I know that he can speak well. And also, behold, he cometh forth to meet thee; and when he seeth thee, he will be glad in his heart. And thou shalt speak unto him, and put words in his mouth: and I will be with thy mouth, and with his mouth, and will teach you what ye shall do." (Exodus 4: 14, 15.) "And the Lord said to Aaron, Go into the wilderness to meet Moses. And he went, and met him in the mount of God, and kissed him. And Moses told Aaron all the words of the Lord who had sent him, and all the signs which he had commanded him." (Exodus 4: 27, 28.)

The World:—When men are called of the Lord, through His inspired servants, to minister unto the people, is it necessary for them to be ordained and set apart for their respective duties by the laying on of the hands of the Lord's servants?

Paul:—It is. Such has been the practice in every Gospel dispensation. Joshua, the son of Nun, was set apart, as directed of the Lord, through the imposition of hands by Moses. Let me read to you what Moses has written on this matter: "And the Lord said unto Moses, take thee Joshua, the son of Nun, a man in whom is the spirit, and lay thine hands upon him; and set him before Eleazar the priest, and before all the congregation; and give him a charge in their sight. And thou shalt put some of thine honor upon him, that all the congregation of the children of Israel may be obedient. * * * And Moses did as the Lord commanded him: and he took Joshua, and set him before Eleazar the priest, and before all the congregation: and he laid his hands upon him, and gave him a charge, as the Lord commanded by the hand of Moses." (Num. 27: 18-20, 22, 23.)

The World:—Paul, in what way were you called to the ministry, and by whom were you ordained?

Paul:—I was called by the Holy Ghost, and was ordained under the hands of Simeon, Lucius and Manaen. You will find a record of my call and ordination in the 13th chapter of the Acts of the Apostles, as follows: "Now there was in the church that was at Antioch certain prophets and teachers; as Barnabas, and Simeon that was called Niger, and Lucius of Cyrene, and Manaen, which had been brought up with Herod the tetrarch, and Saul. As they ministered to the Lord, and fasted, the Holy Ghost said, Separate me Barnabas and Saul for the work whereunto I have called them. And when they had fasted and prayed, and laid their hands on them, they sent them away." (Acts 13: 1-3.)

The World:—We have no further questions to ask you, Paul.

Latter-day Saints:—We now respectfully ask you to hear what the Apostle Peter has to say on this very important matter.

PETER'S TESTIMONY.

The World:—Were you called of the Lord and ordained to take part in His ministry?

Peter:—I was. You will find an account of my call and ordination, as well as that of the other eleven apostles, in the third chapter of Mark's gospel. It is as follows: "And he goeth up into a mountain, and calleth unto him whom he would: and they came unto him. And he ordained twelve, that they should be with him, and that he might send them forth to preach." (Mark 3: 13, 14.) "Ye have not chosen me," said Jesus, "but I have chosen you, and ordained you, that ye should go and bring forth fruit, and that your fruit should remain: that whatsoever you shall ask of the Father in my name, he may give it you." (John 15: 16.)

The World:—Must a man be called of God and ordained by divine authority before he can hold an office in the Church of Christ?

Peter:—He must. The death of Judas left a vacancy in the council of Apostles. In choosing his successor we appealed to the Lord to manifest to us His mind and will in the selection of a man to fill the vacancy. There were two men, Barsabas and Matthias, whom we considered equally worthy of the honor. We presented these two men before the Lord in prayer, and said. "Thou, Lord, which knowest the hearts of all men, show which of these two thou hast chosen. That he may take part of this ministry and apostleship, from which Judas by transgression fell, that he might go to his own place." (Acts 1: 24, 25.) It was manifested to us that Matthias was the Lord's choice, and he was appointed by unanimous vote.

The World:—Are we to understand from what you have said that it was the desire of the Lord that apostles and prophets and all the other officers should continue in the Church?

Peter:—Such, indeed, was the desire of the Lord. If it had not been, He would not have appointed a successor to Judas.

The World:—Our ministers have told us that apostles and prophets are not necessary in these days; that they were placed in the Church to establish Christianity, and that when Christianity was established they were no longer needed.

Peter:—There is nothing in the Scriptures to warrant such an assertion. On the contrary, it is most positively stated that the Lord put these officers in the Church "for the perfecting of the saints, for the work of the ministry, for the edifying of the body of Christ." And they were to remain in the Church "till we all come in the unity of the faith, and of the knowledge of the Son of God, unto a perfect man, unto the measure of the stature of the fulness of Christ; that we henceforth be no more children, tossed to and fro, and carried about with every wind of doctrine, by the sleight of men, and cunning craftiness, whereby they lie in wait to deceive." (Eph. 4: 12-14.)

The World:—How was the primitive Christian Church organized?

Peter:—It was "built upon the foundation of apostles and prophets, Jesus Christ himself being the chief corner stone." (Eph. 2: 20.) The Lord placed in the Church apostles, prophets, evangelists, pastors, teachers, etc. (Eph. 4: 11.)

The World:—The churches of the world are not organized after that pattern?

Peter:—They are not. They were not established by Christ. Had Christ established them, He would have put in them the same officers that He put in the early Christian Church. The churches of the world were established by men. They are named after men. There is Saint Paul's Church, Saint Peter's Church, Saint Mark's Church, Saint Luke's Church, Saint John's Church, etc.

The World:—There seems, therefore, to have been an apostasy from the primitive Christian Church?

Peter:—There has been. The Scriptures are replete with prophecies concerning the great apostasy which was to take place after the death of the apostles. Permit me to call your attention to a few of them. Have you a Bible at hand?

The World:—We have.

Peter:—Turn to the fourth chapter of Paul's second epistle to Timothy and read what he prophesied concerning the apostasy that was to take place.

The World:—Paul prophesied as follows: "For the time will come when they will not endure sound doctrine; but after their own lusts shall they heap to themselves teachers, having itching ears; and they shall turn away their ears from the truth, and shall be turned unto fables." (II Tim. 4: 3, 4.)

Peter:—Now turn to the 29th chapter of Isaiah and read what he said concerning the state of the world in the last days.

The World:—Isaiah prophesied as follows: "Stay yourselves, and wonder: cry ye out, and cry: they are drunken, but not with wine; they stagger, but not with strong drink. For the Lord hath poured out upon you the spirit of deep sleep, and hath closed your eyes: the prophets and your rulers, the seers hath he covered. Wherefore the Lord said, forasmuch as this people draw near me with their mouth, and with their lips do honor me, but have removed their heart far from me, and their fear toward me is taught by the precept of men." (Isaiah 29: 9, 10, 13.)

Peter:—How perfectly did Paul describe the condition of the world at the present time! Instead of having inspired apostles and prophets to reveal to them the mind and will of the Lord, and to teach them the true plan of salvation, the people have heaped to themselves teachers, having itching ears, and they have turned their ears away from the truth and turned them unto fables. When you think of the multitude of jarring and contending sects that are in the world to-day, you can see how literally the prophecies of Paul and Isaiah have been fulfilled.

The World:—Were Paul and Isaiah the only ones who prophecied concerning an apostasy?

Peter:—They were not. There were many others who uttered similar predictions. But I ask you to read what Isaiah further said concerning the apostasy; you will find it in the twenty-fourth chapter of his book.

The World:—Isaiah says: "The earth also is defiled under the inhabitants thereof; because they have transgressed the laws, changed the ordinance, broken the everlasting covenant. Therefore hath the curse devoured the earth, and they that dwell therein are desolate: therefore the inhabitants of the earth are burned, and few men left." (Isaiah 24: 5, 6.)

Peter:—Notice the similarity in these prophecies: Isaiah prophesied that the day would come when the people would transgress the laws, change the ordinance, and break the everlasting covenant. Paul declared that the time would come when they would not endure sound doctrine, but would heap to themselves teachers, have itching ears, and would turn away their ears from the truth and turn them unto fables.

The World:—Are there any other prophecies in the Scriptures foretelling an apostasy?

Peter:—There are many. On another occasion Paul prophesied as follows: "For I know this, that after my departure shall grievous wolves enter in among you, not sparing the flock. Also of your own selves shall men arise, speaking perverse things, to draw away disciples after them." (Acts 20: 29, 30.) Paul lived to see the beginning of the terrible apostasy of which he spoke. "I marvel," said he, writing to the Galatians, "that ye are so soon removed from him that called you into the grace of Christ unto another gospel: which is not another; but there be some that trouble you, and would pervert the gospel of Christ." (Gal 1: 6, 7.) I myself prophesied concerning the apostasy. Here is what I said: "But there were false prophets also among the people, even as there shall be false teachers among you, who privily shall bring in damnable heresies, even denying the Lord that bought them, and bring upon themselves swift destruction. And many shall follow their pernicious ways; by reason of whom the way of truth shall be evil spoken of. And through covetousness shall they with feigned words make merchandise of you." (II. Peter 2: 1-3.)

The World:—The prophets and apostles truly foretold an apostasy, and the divided state of Christendom—the hundreds of different sects and denominations, the numerous, conflicting theories which are being advocated by men for the Gospel of Jesus Christ—bear incontrovertible testimony that such an apostasy has taken place. Must this condition continue, or will there be a restitution?

Peter:—There will be a restitution of all things spoken of by the mouth of the holy prophets.

The World:—Do you think the Lord will ever send us Apostles and Prophets to teach us the true Gospel of Christ as it was taught by Him and His inspired servants in ancient days?

Peter:—He will, for so He has declared. Here is the Apostle John; I pray you, hear what he has to say concerning the restoration of the Gospel in the latter days.

JOHN'S TESTIMONY.

The World:—John, do you think we will ever be favored with new revelation from God?

John:—Have you forgotten what Joel prophesied concerning the last days? He said, "And it shall come to pass afterward, that I will pour out my Spirit upon all flesh; and your sons and your daughters shall prophesy, your old men shall dream dreams, your young men shall see visions." (Joel 2: 28.)

The World:—Then, we may look for prophets to be sent of God.

John:—Yes, and angels also will come down from heaven to restore that which was lost. You have heard already of the great apostasy that was to take place; you have seen how the principles and ordinances of the Gospel have been perverted; you see the Christian world a Babel of confusion. The Lord knew that all these things would take place, and He decreed that in the last days He would set His hand again to recover His people from their lost and fallen state. He revealed to me that before His judgments were poured out upon the inhabitants of the earth He would send an angel with the everlasting Gospel, to be preached to every nation under heaven. Read, I pray you, what I said concerning this matter in the fourteenth chapter of my book.

The World:—You wrote as follows: "And I saw another angel fly in the midst of heaven, having the everlasting Gospel to preach unto them that dwell on the earth, and to every nation, and kindred, and tongue, and people, saying with a loud voice, Fear God, and give glory to him; for the hour of his judgment is come: and worship him that made heaven and earth, and the sea, and the fountains of waters." (Rev. 14: 6, 7.)

John:—Now, I advise you to look for the fulfillment of the things which the Lord has spoken by the mouth of His holy prophets.

The World:—Thank you, John; you are excused.

Latter-day Saints:—Now, we testify to you in words of soberness that the angel which John predicted would come to the earth in the last days with the everlasting Gospel, has come to the Prophet Joseph Smith. The Lord also sent heavenly messengers to him and others, who conferred upon them divine authority, and instructed them concerning the restoration of the true Church of Christ on the earth for the last time, preparatory to the coming of the Son of Man. That Church has been organized after the primitive pattern. In it are inspired apostles and prophets, evangelists, pastors and teachers. It teaches the very same Gospel that was taught by Christ and His Apostles; its members enjoy the same gifts and blessings that were enjoyed by the former-day Saints: they have the gift of prophecy, revelations, visions, healing, tongues, interpretation of tongues, etc. And, if you desire to know the truth of these things, we say, Follow the exhortation of the Apostle James, when he said, "If any of you lack wisdom, let him ask of God, that giveth to all men liberally, and upbraideth not; and it shall be given him." (James 1: 5.)

THURSDAY, JANUARY 31, 1907.

THE NEW THEOLOGY.

CONSIDERABLE agitation has been stirred up in religious circles by a movement that is called "The New Theology." It is described by its promoters as a growth rather than a sudden development. They also deprecate this title, and state that it is not really new, but the expression of views that have been long entertained by many thinking persons in different religious denominations. The prominence which it has recently obtained has been brought about largely by the preaching of the Rev. R. J. Campbell at the City Temple in London, which has attracted large crowds of interested listeners. Mr. Campbell is the successor at that place of the late Dr. Parker, and is a minister of the Congregational church. That body does not appear to repudiate the gentleman or his teachings, and he is evidently supported by a number of ministers in the same denomination.

It is a little difficult, in the midst of the conflicting statements that have been made by preachers and newspapers in reference to The New Theology, to tell what it really is and what are its essential differences to the orthodox creeds of the day. It is not usually safe to depend upon the explanations of any doctrine that are given by its opponents. They are often so different from those expressed by its advocates as to be entirely misleading; this is not always intentionally so, but in religious controversies there is commonly a shade of bitterness with a strong bias, which renders them unreliable. Some very fierce attacks upon the alleged position taken by Mr. Campbell have been made by Episcopal Bishops and by dissenting preachers in different pulpits, but from that which may be gleaned out of the reports of Mr. Campbell's sermons and interviews with newspaper reporters, it is pretty clear that, in the main, his views are as follows:

While he does not fully endorse the name "The New Theology," he tacitly accepts it and uses it in speaking of the movement of which he is, just now, the principal exponent. The starting point in it, as he expresses it, "is belief in the immanence of God and the essential oneness of God and man." It declares that "man is the revelation of God, and the universe a means to the self-manifestation of God." The word "God" thus stands for "the infinite reality whence all things proceed." Mr. Campbell explains: "We believe that there is thus no real distinction between humanity and deity. Our being is the same as God's, although our consciousness of it is limited. We see the revelation of God in everything around us." As to Jesus Christ, He is "the perfect example of what humanity ought to be, the life which perfectly expresses God in our limited human experience." Thus "every man is a potential Christ, or rather a manifestation of the eternal Christ, that side of the nature of God from which all humanity has come forth."

It will be seen from this that the New Theology repudiates the idea of a personal God such as the Being described in the Bible, and also the Biblical doctrine of the Sonship of Christ, so pointedly taught by His apostles and presented as the very foundation of the Christian faith. Further, The New Theology announces that "the seat of religious authority is within, not without, the human soul." This virtually denies directly the doctrine of revelation from God to man, either by His own voice, or by the administration of angels or by any of the methods mentioned in the Scriptures.

Mr. Campbell admits openly that he and his associates "believe that the story of the Fall, in a literal sense, is untrue; that it is literature, not dogma, the romance of an early age used for the ethical instruction of man." Consequently it is to be expected that, as he says, they reject wholly "the common interpretation of the Atonement—that another is beaten for our fault." Also that they believe "not in a final judgment, but in a judgment that is ever proceeding." The doctrine of sin, which holds us to be blameworthy for deeds that we cannot help, Mr. Campbell says, "we believe to be a false view. Sin is simply selfishness. It is an offence against the God within, a violation of the law of love."

After this plain repudiation of the divinity of Christ, singular to say, Mr. Campbell opened one of his meetings by offering a prayer to Jesus Christ. Whether this was for the purpose of falling in with the views of people in his congregation who, through early training or otherwise, are impressed with a feeling of reverence for the crucified Son of Man so that they still hold to the doctrine of salvation by faith in Him, or whether it was from the force of habit we cannot say, but that it was utterly inconsistent with his own explanation of the ideas embodied in The New Theology, appears to us indisputable.

Some of the teachings of Mr. Campbell indicate to the ordinary investigator that they are but new utterances of the theories of Unitarianism. But while there are some of his notions that are in common with Unitarianism, he draws a line of distinction between the two creeds. As he describes it, "Unitarianism made a great gulf and put man on one side and God on the other," while

Mr. Campbell makes no distinctions between man and God, but declares that "our being is the same as God's, but our consciousness of it is limited." Thus, The New Theology goes much farther away than Unitarianism from the Biblical doctrine of God as a personal Being, the Father of us all to whom we should pray and whom we should obey as the Author of our being, the Supreme Ruler of the universe, who sent His Son into the world that all mankind might be saved from sin, through faith in Him and obedience to His commandments; that death came into the world through disobedience to God, which is sin; and that life will be restored to all through the perfect obedience, even unto death, of the world's Redeemer. While Unitarianism spiritualizes away the plain declarations of the Hebrew prophets and the Savior's apostles, it does not entirely throw aside the principle of Deity as distinct from, and sublimely superior to humanity. The New Theology tosses aside the whole doctrine of God, the Father, Christ, the Savior, the responsibility of man to his Maker, the atonement for sin, the resurrection of the dead and the final judgment. How that can be rationally viewed, in any sense, as Christian theology, we are at a complete loss to determine.

The New Theology is one more among the many diversions which the spirit of darkness has used to blind the eyes of the children of men, through false philosophy and vain deceit "after the rudiments of this world and not after Christ." The tendency of modern religious thought has been in channels divergent from the plain and simple "strait and narrow way which leadeth unto life." It offers a smooth and pleasant path for sinners who do not desire to feel their responsibility to a Supreme Power who will ultimately be their Supreme Judge; who wish to be a "law unto themselves"; who would be perfectly free to follow their own inclinations and notions without let or hindrance or the bonds of that which is called conscience. The throngs that are running after the expounders of this new creed, which vainly professes to be merely a restatement of the old theology, gives evidence of the willingness of the multitude to follow after something which will relieve them from the restrictions of divine law and the fear of the consequences of their own transgressions.

It was time that the Eternal Father revealed anew from heaven the everlasting Gospel, manifesting Himself in person with His Son Jesus Christ to the youthful prophet, Joseph Smith, and sending angels once more to earth with those truths that are saving in their nature, and restoring that authority once held by inspired apostles and prophets in former times. "Mormonism," as it is called, is a new witness to mankind that the God of the Bible is, in very deed, the true and living God, who made man in His own image; that Jesus of Nazareth is the Christ; that He died for man's redemption; that sin is the transgression of the laws of God; that all people must eventually give an account for their earthly acts;

that their status in the eternal life will be according to their doings in mortal life; that God will judge the world at the time and times that are fixed in His providence, and that all mankind may come to Christ and be prepared for exaltation in the presence of the Father, through faith and repentance and the new birth of water and of the Spirit, and continuance in observing His commandments and living by every word that proceedeth from the mouth of God. This is the truth before God and man, and will stand the test both of reason and Scripture, notwithstanding all the theories and notions of man's invention or proceeding from the realms of darkness, whether they be the vagaries of olden times or described now as "The New Theology."

C. W. P.

Stars Wanted.—The mission is in need of a few copies of numbers 1 and 31 of the MILLENNIAL STAR for 1906. These are required in order to complete volumes, and those who can spare the above numbers would confer a great favor by sending them to this office.

Scottish Conference.—The Scottish Conference will be held in Glasgow, at Gordon Halls, 316 Paisley Road, at 10:30 a.m., and 2 and 6 p.m., on Sunday, February 10th, 1907. President Charles W. Penrose will be present, with the President and Elders of the conference.

Deseret News Appeals for Aid in Behalf of Sufferers in China.— In response to a letter of appeal from the American National Red Cross Association, Washington, D. C., of which the Hon. William Taft is president, the *Deseret News* has appealed, both in its editorial and news columns, to the people of Utah to subscribe to a cash relief fund in behalf of famine sufferers in China. Some time ago, when a similar appeal was made in behalf of starving multitudes in Japan, the people of the Beehive State were among the first to hasten to their assistance. Even the children in the Sunday Schools and Religion Classes brought the nickles and dimes which they had saved and gave them to the superintendents with the request that they forward them for the relief of their little brothers and sisters far across the sea. The people of China can rest assured that the appeal which the *Deseret News* has made to the citizens of Utah in their behalf will not go unheeded but will be liberally responded to. All subscriptions will be receipted for and forwarded to Hon. Charles Hallam Keep, Red Cross treasurer, room 341 War Department, Washington, D.C.

THE flower by the roadside, that catches the dust of every traveler, is not the one to be admired, and is seldom if ever plucked; but the one blooming away up on the hillside, protected by a perpendicular cliff, is the flower with the virgin perfume, the one that the boy will almost risk his life to possess.

REMARKABLE CASES OF HEALING.

THE following account of a remarkable case of healing was translated from the Dutch *Star* for this magazine by President Alex. Nibley:

Little John, the eleven-year-old son of sister H—— S—— of the Rotterdam branch, had suffered greatly for a number of years with his eyes. They were badly inflamed and pained him continually. He was slowly losing his sight and was unable to attend school longer.

When on a certain day in the beginning of last August it was announced in Rotterdam that President Joseph F. Smith would be in the city the following day and attend meeting, little John said to his mother: "The prophet has the most power of any missionary on earth. If you will take me with you to meeting and he will look into my eyes I believe they will be healed."

According to his desire he was permitted to accompany his mother to the meeting, at the close of which President Smith moved to the door in order to shake hands with the Saints and friends as they passed out of the hall. As the little fellow approached him, led by his mother, and his eyes bandaged with cloths, President Smith took him by the hand and spoke to him kindly. He then raised the bandage slightly and looked sympathetically into the inflamed eyes, at the same time saying something in English which the child could not understand.

The little fellow was satisfied. The prophet had acted according to his faith; and according to his faith so did it come to pass with him. Upon reaching home he cried out: "Mamma, my eyes are well; I can't feel any more pain. I can see fine now, and far, too."

Since then his sight has been good. He attends school again, and one would never think that anything had ever ailed his eyes.

––––––––

SISTER MAUD STEVENS, of the North London branch, writes:

The other day I took up a newspaper, and the words "cured at last" caught my eye. They referred to some patent medicine which was advertised, for which some one had given a testimonial to the effect that after trying many remedies and being "given up" by several doctors, he had at last found something to cure him of his disease. This led me to think of my own marvelous cure, which I am desirous of making public in the hope it may help to benefit other poor sufferers. For many years I had been troubled with a terrible complaint, epilepsy, and had been attended by various doctors, both privately and in hospital, who all prescribed the same remedy, which was in reality as bad or worse than the disease, insomuch as it warded off the fits only to weaken the brain, and to leave other ill effects. After I had embraced the "Mormon" faith about eighteen months, I read in the STAR of a lady who had been cured of the same complaint, and I spoke to Elder Charles H. Smith, who was the instrument in the hands of the Lord in bringing me into the fold of Jesus Christ. He promised me that I should also be cured, and asked me if I then had sufficient faith to leave off taking the medicine which had become to me such a necessity. I told him I was afraid I had not, and it was not until nearly six months later that I obtained it. Even then my faith was of such a poor, weak nature that for days I went about in fear and trembling; but by the grace of God and continual prayer it grew gradually, until to-day my heart goes up in thankfulness to my Heavenly Father for having healed me of my awful affliction, and I can sing with my whole heart, "I will praise my God while I have my being."

UNCONSCIOUS GREATNESS.

MANY of the achievements of men which are now regarded as great, when they were wrought in life's common ways did not appear to have anything remarkable in them. Their authors did not themselves dream of the far-reaching importance of what they had done, or of the fame which in after ages would gather about their names. Many discoverers and inventors would be bewildered if they were to come back to earth to-day and find their names perpetuated in halls of fame and see how large a place the things they did now fill in the world's life.

Many of those to whom the world owes the most wrought obscurely, in poverty ofttimes, sacrificing themselves, toiling, suffering, in order to perfect their invention or complete their discovery. They saw nothing great or splendid in what they were doing. In many cases their lives seemed failures, for they were only pioneers and achieved nothing themselves. Others came after them and carried to perfection what they had striven in vain to accomplish. To-day the things they dreamed of but never realized are among the world's finest achievements, its most useful inventions. If they are told in the judgment that these great things were wrought by them they will answer that they never saw them. It will be true, too, for what they saw were only the merest beginnings, the first rude attempts, from which the finished product came only after years of experimenting. No wonder they cannot recognize in the splendid results the little that their hands actually wrought. Yet all this is really their work, was born in their brain, and made possible only through their dream and self-denying devotion.

So it is of the deeds of kindness that good people do. Those who do them never think of them as worthy of commendation, much less of record. They are plain people, with only commonplace gifts, with no aspiration for fame, with no thought that anything they do is of any special importance or will ever be heard of again. Yet in many of these lowly ministries Christ sees the beginning of something that will shine at length in heavenly splendor. A simple word of cheer puts hope into a discouraged heart, saves a life from despair, and starts it on a career of worthy service.

A sailor boy brought home a fuchsia to his mother from some foreign cruise. She put it in a window box and it grew, and by its beauty drew attention to itself. Soon there were fuchsias in other neighboring windows and in countless gardens. Thus the one little plant which the boy brought over seas multiplied itself and spread everywhere. If on the judgment day the Master shows this boy fuchsias growing in gardens, in window boxes, in conservatories in many lands, and says, "you planted all these; all this beauty is from your hand," the boy will be overwhelmed with surprise. He never saw these thousands of blooming plants. "Lord, when did I plant all these?" But we understand it. His hand brought one little plant, in love, from a foreign land, and the one has multiplied into all this vast harvest of loveliness.—REV. J. R. MILLER, in *The Family Herald.*

MARRIAGE.

A WRITER in the *Purity Advocate* says: "People take great care to match horses and other animals, in order to maintain a pure and vigorous lineage. Little or no care is taken on this score when contracting marriage. A young woman heedlessly marries into a family known to be affected with some hereditary disease, never reflecting, until too late, on the consequences of her act. She forgets that, in a physical as well as in a mental sense, the sins of the fathers are apt to be visited upon the children.

'Can troubled or polluted springs
A hallowed stream afford?'

"Indisputably they cannot, and the fact should be borne in mind in the matter of courtship. Let not the institution of marriage be charged with calamity. Your own rash conduct in forming the alliance is at fault. We may be sorry for you in the trying circumstances, but the penalty of indiscretion is inevitable."

The Vicar of Wakefield tells us that he chose his wife as she chose her wedding gown, which was on the principle of selecting one that would wear well. If in the article of marriage you fix on a flimsy material, take the consequences, and blame nobody but yourself. The market is open. Do not be in a hurry. Yet, do not put off the time because you happen to be unable to start a high scale of worldly wealth. Early marriages may not always be commendable, but waiting to reach some imaginary standard is— all other things being equal—by no means sound policy.

FROM THE MISSION FIELD.

Arrivals.—The following Elders arrived in Liverpool, January 26th, 1907, per s.s. *Cymric*: For Great Britain—Richard S. Ballantyne, Logan; Walter Caldwell, Caldwell, Alberta, Canada; Edwin Crockett, Preston, Idaho; Charles A. Duke, Raymond, Canada; Edward Lublin, Spring Coulee, Canada; Reginald Evans, Kemmerer, Wyoming; Joseph K. Udall, Eagar, Arizona. For Scandinavia—Hyrum Hansen, Spanish Fork; Henry Ole Olson, Joseph H. Hansen, Brigham City; Anton Jensen, Weston, Idaho; Martin Jensen, Jr., Richfield; James P. Rasmussen, Millville. For Sweden—Alfred F. Anderson, Grover, Wyo.; Carl Victor E. Krantz, Salt Lake City. For Switzerland and Germany—Charles L. Angerbauer, Brigham City; George H. Dubois, Spanish Fork; Jacob R. Fuhrimann, Logan; Paul E. B. Hammer, Sr., Salt Lake City; Simon Hugentobler, Salina; John H. Murri, Midway.

Appointments.—The Elders who arrived for the British mission, January 26th, 1907, have been appointed to labor in the following conferences: Richard S. Ballantyne, Scottish; Walter Caldwell, Newcastle; Edwin Crockett, Liverpool; Charles A. Duke, Manchester; Edward Lublin, Nottingham; Reginald Evans, Birmingham; Joseph K. Udall, London.

SUNDAY SCHOOL LESSON FOR THEOLOGICAL DEPARTMENT.
Lesson for February 10, 1907.
JESUS THE CHRIST.

LESSON 1.—INTRODUCTORY.

1. Names and Titles. (a) Definition of each. (b) Names given of God are likewise titles. (c) "Jesus," "Christ," and "Messiah."

2. The Savior's name made known before His birth. (a) At the annunciation (Luke 1: 31, see also 2: 21; Matt. 1: 21, 25, see also verse 23 and compare Isaiah 7: 14; Luke 2: 11.) (b) To ancient psophets (*Moses 6: 51, 56; 7: 50; 8: 24; Isa. 7: 14; I Nephi 10: 4; II Nephi 10: 3; Mosiah 3: 8.)

3. The man, Jesus. (a) A mortal being; birth, human condition, and death. (b) His mission in mortality. (See Moses 1: 6; 4: 1-3; 6: 52, and references thereto.) (c) Son of mortal mother and immortal Father.

4. Christ, the Lord. (a) His resurrection to immortality. (b) One of the Godhead. (Acts 1: 33; Phil. 2: 9-11; Heb. 10: 12; III Nephi 11: 8-11; Doc. and Cov. 1: 20; 6: 2, 7; 10: 57-70.)

Suggestions:—Significance of names given of God may be illustrated by other examples: Ishmael (Gen. 16: 11); John (Luke 1: 13); Abraham (Gen. 17: 5); Sarah (Gen. 17: 15); Israel (Gen. 32: 28; 35: 10); Peter (Matt. 16: 18; Luke 6: 14; John 1: 42.)

* Pearl of Great Price.

"STAND LIKE AN ANVIL."

"Stand like an anvil," said a saint,
When a dear brother made complaint
Of woes and wrongs that he had borne
By which his life was worn and torn.
Though ready at his Maker's will
His holy duty to fulfill,
His heart could not fail to be broken
By poisoned words in anger spoken,
And by malignant deeds they came
From scorn's or hate's satanic flame.

"Stand like an anvil," bravely bear
All blows that injury can dare
To shower upon thee with a hand
That rancor's venom does command.
"Stand like an anvil," when to foes
Turn friends and fiercely beat with blows.
Incessant, harder, more and more,
For the dear love that was before.
In all this world the hardest fate
Is that where love is turned to hate.

"Stand like an anvil," when the strong
In tones of mad, defiant wrong
Will thee with pounding hammers smite
For daring to defend the right.
"Stand like an anvil;" never quail
Though persecutions strike like hail,
For every stroke adds one more ray
To thy bright crown in endless day.

"Stand like an anvil;" so true be
To God whatever comes to thee.
"Stand like an anvil," then shalt thou
Stand like an angel, and shalt bow
Before the throne of gladness bright
In heaven's domain of fadeless light.

SELECTED.

CONTENTS:

EDITED, PRINTED AND PUBLISHED BY CHARLES W. PENROSE, 295 EDGE LANE,
LIVERPOOL:
FOR SALE IN ALL THE CONFERENCES OF THE CHURCH OF JESUS CHRIST OF
LATTER-DAY SAINTS IN GREAT BRITAIN.